Young Readers' Series

Captain Jim and the KILLER WHALES

Carol A. Amato
Illustrated by Patrick O'Brien

BARRON'S

Dedication
To Chris, who asks the best questions

All inquiries should be addressed to:
Barron's Educational Series, Inc.
250 Wireless Boulevard
Hauppauge, New York 11788

International Standard Book No. 0-8120-9289-9

Library of Congress Catalog Card No. 95-13657

Library of Congress Cataloging-in-Publication Data

Amato, Carol A.
    Captain Jim and the Killer Whales / Carol A. Amato;
illustrated by Patrick O'Brien.
        p.   cm.—(Young readers' series)
    ISBN 0-8120-9289-9
    1. Killer whale—Juvenile literature. [1. Killer whale.]
I. O'Brien, Patrick, 1960– ill. II. Title. III. Series: Amato, Carol A. Young readers' series.
QL737.C432A535 1995
599.5'3—dc20   95-13657
                                                                            CIP
                                                                            AC

PRINTED IN HONG KONG
5678   9955   9876543

Table of Contents

Mandy turned her head on her pillow. She opened one eye. She could see the sun shining through the sides of the shade.

"It must be time to get up," she thought. "Too bad it's a school day," she said out loud.

Just then her twin brother Zach ran into the room.
"Get up, Mandy!" he shouted.

"Shhh! I'm not awake yet," Mandy said.

"Did you forget?" said Zach. "Today is the first day of summer vacation!"

"Wow! I *did* forget! Let's go!"

Zach and Mandy had been waiting for this day. They knew what they wanted to do. Captain Jim would be waiting for them.

They both ate their breakfast as fast as they could.

"Slow down!" their mother said. "You have all summer!"

Soon they were running down the road to the dock. They came to the "Boats and Bait" shop. Captain Jim was sitting on a bench outside, mending fishing nets.

"Hi, Captain Jim!" they both said.

"We're back!" said Mandy.

"So you are," said Captain Jim, "and it's good to see you!"

"It's good to see *you*, too!" said Zach.

"I'll bet you'd like to hear some new stories about the sea."

"Yes!" Zach and Mandy said at the same time.

Captain Jim had been the captain of his own fishing boat. He had worked at sea most of his life, even when he was a boy. He had many stories to tell about his life at sea.

"What will you tell us about today?" asked Mandy.

"As you know, when we were fishing out at sea, we saw many animals. Some flew in the air. Some swam in the sea. Some lived on islands. We caught many kinds of animals in our big nets."

"Last summer you told us about the sharks that got caught in the nets," said Zach. "You said the fishermen were not fishing for sharks!"

"Yes," said the Captain. "Do you remember some of the other things we talked about?"

"I remember," said Mandy. "You told us that many people are afraid of sharks."

"That's because there are some scary movies and TV shows about sharks," said Zach.

"That's right," said the Captain.

7

"There are also good movies, TV shows, and books about sharks. Many people do not see or know about these. They often *do* see the scary things.

"It is a good thing to be afraid when a wild animal is near. No one can tell what a wild animal might do when *it* becomes afraid. Wild animals may attack to protect themselves or their babies.

"Most people think all sharks are dangerous. This is not true. When sharks do attack, they are doing what sharks do best, being one of the top predators in the sea. Do you remember what a predator is?"

"A predator hunts and eats other animals," said Mandy. "A shark may eat a large fish. The large fish may eat a smaller fish. The smaller fish may eat an even smaller fish. The . . ."

"OK, OK! We get the point!" said her brother.

"But she's right," laughed Captain Jim. "The shark plays an important part in this food chain."

Some animals eat plants. Some eat other animals. Others eat plants *and* animals. Most animals eat more than one thing, so the food chain becomes more like a food web. Animals become connected to one another like a web by what they need to eat. They all depend upon each other to live and grow. A food chain or web tells about who eats what."

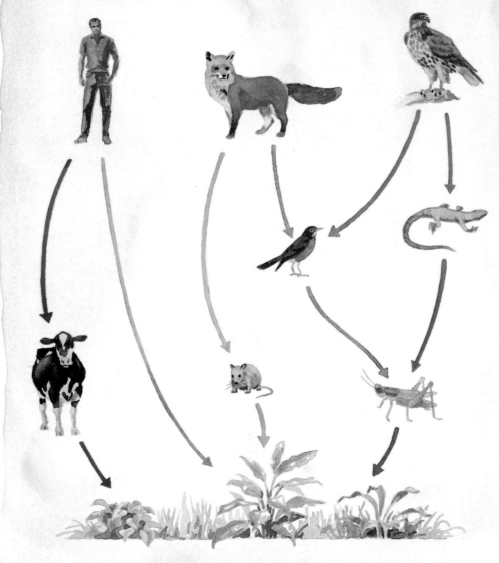

"Today I want to tell you about another top predator in the sea—the killer whale," said Captain Jim.

"Many people think killer whales are mean and dangerous. Like sharks, there have been many scary stories about them. Most of these stories are not true. Like the shark, the killer whale has been given a bad name."

"Then why are they called *killer* whales?" asked Zach.

"They were given the name 'killer' many years ago because of the way they hunt. Many people thought they were the most dangerous animals in the sea. Stories tell of their attacks on small boats. None of these stories were ever proved.

"Killer whales *did* attack some people! In faraway cold places, people standing on the ice have been attacked by killer whales. There is a reason for this. Seals and penguins can be found on the ice, too. Killer whales hunt seals and penguins. The whale tries to smash the ice. It tries to get the animal into the water. The whale cannot see well out of the water. It may think a person is a seal or a penguin. Killer whales do not eat people. They are wild animals that feed on other wild animals."

"Many people feed on other animals, too. Where do people get meat and fish to eat?" Captain Jim asked the children.

"Not on the ice!" laughed Zach.

"Yes sir . . . they might be ice fishing!" said Mandy.

"Sure, but we can get our fish and meat in stores . . . and some people hunt animals," said Zach.

"Yes," said the Captain. "Like wild animals, we eat what we eat so that we can live."

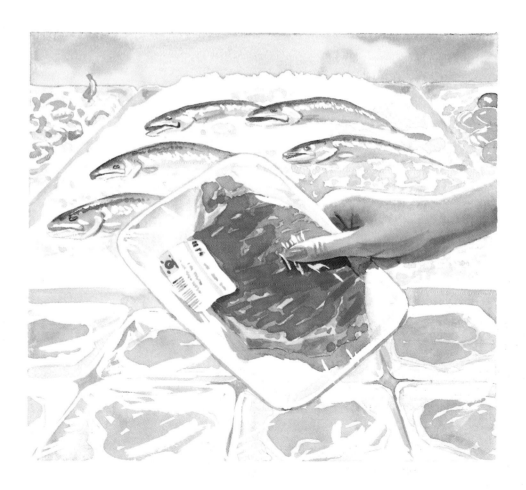

"Are killer whales like other kinds of whales?" asked Zach.

"In some ways," said Captain Jim. "Like the other whales, they are mammals. Mammals must breathe air. Their babies are born alive. They drink milk from their mothers. They have fur or hair.

"We are mammals, too, and like you, Zach, whales have very little hair!"

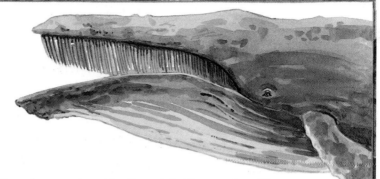

"Killer whales have teeth," said Captain Jim.

"Some whales have baleen instead of teeth. Baleen is like a big strainer. It strains small fish and tiny sea life out of the sea.

"Whales with teeth, like the killer, are hunters. They are in the dolphin family. All dolphins have teeth."

"Does that mean that the killer whale is a kind of dolphin?" asked Mandy.

"That's right," said the Captain. "It is the largest dolphin in the sea. Scientists named the killer whale 'orca.'"

"Can we call it 'orca,' too?" asked Zach. "'Killer' sounds so mean!"

"Sure!" said the Captain. "Scientists want to learn more about orcas and so do we!"

"When I was a fisherman," began Captain Jim, "I saw many orcas in the sea. During all those years, I learned many things about them. Orcas can be found in all of the seas of the world. They like the cold seas best. There is more food in the colder seas. The orcas would swim right up to our boat."

"Were there many of them?" asked Zach.

"There were 10, 20, and even more in a pod," said the Captain.

"What's a pod?" asked Mandy. "I thought only peas were in a pod!"

"Well, I guess you could say that the peas in the pod make a family of peas!" said the Captain.

"The whales in a pod are like a family of whales. The orcas eat, sleep, and play in the family pod. They act like a family, too. They help each other when they are sick or hurt. They hunt together, too. Together, they can hunt whales much bigger than they are.

"Each orca knows its place and job in the pod.

"The males (boys) are called bulls, the females (girls) are cows, and the babies are calves."

"Do they *moo*?" asked Mandy.

"Very funny!" said Zach.

"They *do* make many kinds of sounds," said Captain Jim. "Some of these sounds help dolphins find things in the water. These are short click-click-clicking sounds. These sounds bounce off of things. This lets the dolphin find out what is around it in the sea.

"Scientists think orcas and other dolphins have ways to 'talk' to each other."

"Talking whales?" asked Mandy.

"Oh, no!" laughed Captain Jim. "They don't talk as we do!"

"Dolphins and whales make whistles, squeaks, barks, and many high and low sounds. We do not know what they are 'saying' to each other. These sounds may be a way to keep the pod close. They may teach or warn or tell about feelings. Some whales seem to be singing."

"Can they sing like us?" asked Zach.

"I hope not like *you*!" laughed Mandy.

"Not like *any* of us!" said Captain Jim.

"Their songs are made up of many sounds. They are beautiful to hear. Scientists study these songs to try to find out what these sounds mean. Some scientists think orcas sing, too."

"Did you ever see orcas up close, Captain Jim?" asked Zach.

"Yes," he said, "and I will tell you about one of these times!"

Chapter 5

The Calf

"One day in the summer, our fishing boat was far out at sea," began Captain Jim. "We could tell a storm was coming. The sky was getting darker and darker and the wind was blowing. We started to take the nets in. It was hard work because the sea was rough.

"All of a sudden we heard a squeal! Then another. The squeals got higher and louder. One of the men called out, 'A killer whale is caught in the net!'

"We all ran to the stern, which is in the back of the boat. An orca calf was caught in the net. It was fighting to free itself. The more it fought, the more caught it became. It was a small calf, about 400 pounds (about 180 kilograms) and about 8 feet (about 2 meters) long. Orca calves are just a little smaller than this when they are born. We knew it was very young."

"We could see the mother orca a few feet away. She swam back and forth and around the net. Then she dove under the net. She did not know what to do to help her calf. Mother orcas take good care of their babies. They have only one calf at a time. A baby is born only every three years or so. The mother and calf are very close. If a calf is hurt or killed, the mother will often swim around it for many days."

"Could she help her baby?" asked Zach.

"No," said Captain Jim, "but *we* did! We lifted up the net with long poles and the baby swam free! The two of them swam away. Soon we could see them diving and breaching in the water."

"What's 'breaching?'" asked Mandy.

"I know," said Zach. "My class went on a 'whale watch' this year. We saw a whale breaching. It's when a whale jumps high out of the water!"

"Right, Zach," said the Captain. "Orcas can also dive to 1,000 feet (about 305 meters). They can stay under water for 20 minutes. They are one of the fastest swimmers in the sea."

"I had the flu and couldn't go on the whale watch!" said Mandy. "I've only seen pictures of some other whales. What does an orca look like?"

"I have some pictures inside the boathouse," said Captain Jim. "Come inside, and I'll show you!"

The boathouse was dark and cool. Zach and Mandy sat down on the old wood chairs while the Captain looked for the orca pictures.

"How long do orcas live?" asked Mandy.

"Scientists are not sure. They think they can live from 25 to 35 years," said Captain Jim.

"How big can they get?" Zach asked.

"A grown-up male is about 23 feet (7 meters). A female, about 20 feet (6 meters). Once we saw one that was about 30 feet (9 meters), which is about as large as they can grow. Like all animals, there are many size differences.

"Now, where did I put those pictures?" he said.

"What do orcas eat?" asked Mandy.

"You both sure do ask a lot of questions," laughed the Captain.

"Orcas eat many kinds of fish. They eat other animals too such as squids, penguins, seals, sea lions, walruses, sea otters, and even other dolphins. The orca is the only dolphin that will eat other dolphins.

"An orca eats about 250 pounds (113 kilograms) of food a day.

"It has about 50 very sharp teeth. They use their teeth to hold and tear, not to chew. They swallow most of their food whole."

"They can swallow those big whales whole?!" asked Zach.

"I was about to say, but *not* the large whales! Some orca meals *can* be pretty big. They may swallow a whole seal!

"At last, *here* they are!" said the Captain, holding up the pictures.

Captain Jim brought the pictures to the table where the twins were sitting.

"Wow!" said Zach.

"It's so beautiful!" Mandy said.

"And *more* than beautiful! Let's look at the orca from head to tail to see what an amazing animal it is," said the Captain.

"As you can see, the orca's back and sides are jet black. Its belly is white. It has a white spot above and behind each eye."

"How much do they weigh?" asked Zach.

"The males can weigh about 9 tons. The females weigh less at about 5 tons. But as I told you, no two animals are the same. Some weigh more and some weigh less.

"Orcas and other sea mammals have blubber to keep them warm. This blubber is fat that is under the skin. The skin is very smooth and does not have much hair."

Chapter 7

It's All In Its Head

Captain Jim pointed to the orca's head.

"Orca's brain is very large. Trainers in aquariums say that they learn fast and are very smart."

"How do they train them?" asked Mandy.

"The aquarium trainers have many ways of training orcas. One way goes something like this:

"The trainer watches the animal. When the animal does something the trainer wants, he or she blows a whistle or uses a hand sign. The sound or sign is repeated each time the animal does what the trainer wants. The animal is given a bit of food each time. It often takes many days or even weeks for the animal to learn this."

Captain Jim showed them another picture. He pointed to the orca's eyes.

"Orca's eyes are small. It can see better under the water than above."

"I don't see any ears," said Zach.

"The orca does not have outside ears as we do. It does have a small opening in the skin. This opening leads to its inside ears. It can hear sounds in the water quite well."

"Where's the orca's nose? Is it small or hidden?" asked Mandy.

"The orca doesn't have a nose, but it does have something like a nose. It has a blowhole." The Captain pointed to the top of the whale's head.

"A whale has lungs. Before it dives, it takes in air through its blowhole. It fills its lungs with as much air as it can. We breathe with lungs, too! When the orca comes to the top of the water, it blows the air out of its blowhole."

"I'm learning to swim," said Mandy. "I fill up my lungs with air before I dive, too!"

"How do you think orca swims?" asked Captain Jim.

"Well, it must use those flippers," Mandy said, pointing to the flippers behind the orca's head, "but what do the flippers do?"

"The flippers are used to help balance, steer, and stop. They are very wide."

"They look like paddles," Zach said.

"Very big paddles. The male's may be 6 feet (2 meters) long and 4 feet (1 meter) wide!

"The large fin on top is called the dorsal fin. The male's dorsal fin is shaped like a triangle. The female's is curved on top. The dorsal fin helps to keep the whale steady while it's swimming.

"The male's dorsal fin is the tallest of all whales, 6 feet (2 meters) high!"

"We didn't talk about this big tail," said Mandy, pointing to the picture.

"You're right!" said the Captain. "The whale's tail is called its flukes. The flukes may be 9 feet (3 meters) wide. They move up and down when the whale swims. Flukes help the whale to swim fast, up to 30 miles per hour! A car driving in the city may go about that fast!"

"Flippers, flukes, and fin," said Mandy. "All of them begin with the letter 'f.' That will be easy to remember!"

"I wish we could see an orca," said Zach.

"Someday you may," said Captain Jim. "Sometimes we can't see some of the animals that live far from us. Still, we must protect them."

"What do you mean, Captain Jim?" asked Mandy.

"In the past, many sea mammals such as seals, sea lions, walruses, whales, and dolphins were hunted. People wanted their fur, meat, and oil. They used their body parts for many other things, too. For years and years they were killed. Many kinds of whales and seals became endangered."

"What does 'endangered' mean?" asked Zach.

"When an animal becomes endangered, it means there are not many left. When the last ones of that kind die, there will be no more. Killing these sea mammals is now against the law."

"Did people hunt orcas?" asked Mandy.

"Orcas were lucky," said the Captain. "They were smaller than the other whales and hard to find, so were not hunted.

"Orcas and other sea life are more in danger today. Our seas are not always clean. Many other kinds of sea animals are killed for food and other things people use.

"People often do not care about what may happen to our seas. If we are not careful, a lot of sea life may die. Animals may not be able to depend upon one another for food.

"We must protect our seas now."

"How can we help?" asked Zach.

"Keep learning and caring about the world around you. When you are grown up, you will be ready to help because you care!

"Oh my, it's way past lunchtime! Will I see you both tomorrow?"

"Oh yes!" Mandy and Zach said at the same time.

"Thanks, Captain Jim, for telling us about the orcas," said Mandy.

And Zach said, "We will always care!"

Glossary

aquarium (a-QUAR-i-um)   a place where people can see and learn about plants and animals that live in the water. An aquarium is also a tank or other kind of container that holds water plants and animals. Some people have aquarium tanks in their homes.

attack (at-TACK)   a sudden act of force by a person or an animal.

balance (BAL-ance)   when two forces are the same. The orca's flippers balance it in the sea so that it will not roll from side to side when it is swimming.

baleen (ba-LEEN)   fills the mouths of whales. It hangs down like fringes in two rows. When the whale's mouth is opened, it takes in large amounts of water. When it closes its mouth, the baleen plates fold backward. The plates form a huge strainer which catch thousands of tiny plants and animals (plankton) and are then swallowed.

blowhole (BLOW-hole)   the nose of the dolphin or whale that is on top of its head. These animals have lungs and must breathe air at the surface of the water. Before diving, they fill their lungs with air. They can shut the hole while diving with a muscle that is like a lip. When they surface to breathe, they let out the air (exhale). This is called the "blow" and is a cloud of steam.

blubber (BLUB-ber) the thick layer of fat between the skin and muscle of whales and other sea mammals. This fat keeps the animal warm. Blubber can be stored as food during times when the animal cannot find much food.

breaching (BREACH-ing) many whales breach, but the orca's breaching is amazing! The 4 to 10 ton animal shoots about 20 feet (6 meters) into the air. It then falls back on its belly, side, or back. Sometimes the whale twists its body during a breach. It may also flip in mid-air and reenter the water head first.

dangerous (DAN-ger-ous) when something can be harmful.

dorsal fin (DOR-sal fin) on the back of sea animals such as fish, dolphins, and whales. The dorsal fin of a male orca may reach 6 feet (2 meters) and is straight; the female's curves toward its back. This fin is used to keep the animal steady while it is swimming. The orca's dorsal fin is the tallest of all whales.

echolocation (ech-o-lo-CA-tion): {not in text} to find and herd their food, orcas use echolocating clicks. These sounds hit something in the water (such as a fish or a rock) and return to the dolphin like an echo. In this way, the dolphin can tell what is around it in the water.

endangered (en-DAN-gered) few of a kind left in the
world. This may happen for reasons we cannot
help. Most often, plants and animals become
endangered when people are not careful. People
may build something in an animal's habitat (place
to live) or they may not keep the wilderness or
ocean clean (pollute). They may kill too many
plants or animals for food or other things people
use . . . like fur coats; they may kill too many for
sport or because they fear the animal. Endangered
animals can become extinct (ex-TINCT). When this
happens, its kind dies out forever. The loss of this
living thing may also endanger the balance of the
food chain of other animals.

female (FE-male) the girls or women in any animal
group, including humans.

flippers (FLIP-pers) found behind the orca's head.
They are used as paddles to help balance, steer,
and stop. The thick and wide paddle-shaped male
flippers may be over 6 feet (2 meters) long and 4
feet (1 meter) wide. They are black above and white
below.

flukes the tail lobes of a whale. They are moved up
and down when the whale swims. When the whale
wants to move quickly, it moves its flukes quickly.
It can swim up to 30 miles (48 kilometers) per hour.
The orca's wide flukes may be 9 feet (3 meters) from
tip to tip.

food chain or web   tells about who eats what (or whom!). A food chain might begin when a large animal eats a smaller animal and that smaller animal eats an even smaller animal. For example, a shark may eat smaller fish, the fish may eat mussels, the mussels may eat plankton. Some food chains get very complicated. These are called food webs because so many animals are part of the web of who eats what (or whom).

island (IS-land . . . the "s" is silent)   land that is surrounded by water on all sides.

killer whale   Orcinus orca (Or-CIN-us OR-ca) or orca for short. Orca is a "toothed" whale. There are two groups of whales: toothed whales and baleen whales. Toothed whales are hunters and have teeth. Baleen whales have baleen and eat plankton. All dolphins are toothed whales. This means that orca is in the dolphin family. Orca is the largest dolphin in the world.)

lungs   two organs with which mammals breathe. The lungs are inside the chest near the heart. They provide the blood with air (oxygen).

male   the boys or men in any animal group, including humans.

mammals (MAM-mals)   animals that breathe air, give birth to live young, drink (nurse) their mother's milk, have the same body temperature all the time, and have some kind of fur or hair.

pod   the orca pod or group is like a very large family. The pod may have 5 to 20 orcas. They often travel and hunt together. The mother (cow) and baby (calf) are very close. The calf may stay close to its mother for up to 10 years, even when new calves are born.

predator (PRED-a-tor)   an animal that kills other animals for food.

protect (pro-TECT)   to keep safe from danger. Also, to stop something from happening: We wear a raincoat to protect ourselves from getting wet.

scientist (SCI-en-tist)   a person who tries to find answers, solve problems, and make discoveries. A scientist does this by asking questions, collecting information, observing findings, and experimenting with ideas, and in many other ways.

trainer (TRAIN-er)   a person who teaches animals (and people, too!). Trainers of captive animals may work in zoos, circuses, aquariums, and other places. They train animals such as dolphins, whales, lions, horses, and others. They teach by using whistles, hand signs, and other signals. It often takes a long time to train an animal just to do one thing.

triangle (TRI-an-gle)   a figure with three sides that are connected at angles.

Dear Parents and Educators:

Welcome to the Young Readers' series!

These learning stories have been created to introduce young children to the study of animals.

Children's earliest exposure to reading is usually through fiction. Stories read aloud invite children into the world of words and imagination. If children are read to frequently, this becomes a highly anticipated form of entertainment. Often that same pleasure is felt when children learn to read on their own. Nonfiction books are also read aloud to children but generally when they are older. However, interest in the "real" world emerges early in life, as soon as children develop a sense of wonder about everything around them.

There are a number of excellent read-aloud natural-science books available. Educators and parents agree that children love nonfiction books about animals. Unfortunately, there are very few that can be read *by* young children. One of the goals of the Young Readers' series is to happily fill that gap!

Captain Jim and the Killer Whales is one in a series of learning stories designed to appeal to young readers. In the classroom, the series can be incorporated into literature-based or whole-language programs, and would be especially suitable for science theme teaching units. Within planned units, each book may serve as a springboard to immersion techniques that include hands-on activities, field study trips, and additional research and reading. Many of the books are also concerned with the threatened or endangered status of the species studied and the role even young people can play in the preservation plan.

These books can also serve as read-alouds for young children. Weaving information through a story form lends itself easily to reading aloud. Hopefully, this book and others in the series will provide entertainment and wonder for both young readers and listeners.

C.A.

In the Classroom

One of the goals of this series is to introduce the young child to factual information related to the species being studied. The science terminology used is relevant to the learning process for the young student. In the classroom, you may want to use multi-modality methods to ensure understanding and word recognition. The following suggestions may be helpful:

1. Refer to the pictures when possible for difficult words and discuss how these words can be used in another context.

2. Encourage the children to use word and sentence contextual clues when approaching unknown words. They should be encouraged to use the glossary since it is an important information adjunct to the story.

3. After the children read the story or individual chapter, you may want to involve them in discussions using a variety of questioning techniques:

   a. Questions requiring *recall* ask the children about past experiences, observations, or feelings. (*Have you ever seen movies or TV programs about whales?*)

   b. *Process* questions help the children to discover relationships by asking them to compare, classify, infer, or explain. (*Do you have to eat every day? Does the whale? Why or why not?*)

   c. *Application* questions ask children to use new information in a hypothetical situation by evaluating, imagining, or predicting. (*In what ways would a lateral line help you?*)

At Home

The above aids can be used if your child is reading independently or aloud. Children will also enjoy hearing this story read aloud to them. You may want to use some of the questioning suggestions above. The story may provoke many questions from your child. Stop and answer the questions. Replying with an honest, "I don't know," provides a wonderful opportunity to head for the library to do some research together!

Have a wonderful time in your shared quest of discovery learning!

Carol A. Amato
Language-Learning Specialist